THE SOMNAMBULIST COOKBOOK

Andrew McDonnell
The Somnambulist Cookbook

SALT

CROMER

PUBLISHED BY SALT PUBLISHING 2019

2 4 6 8 10 9 7 5 3 1

First published in Great Britain in 2019 by
Salt Publishing Ltd
12 Norwich Road, Cromer, Norfolk NR27 0AX United Kingdom

www.saltpublishing.com

Salt Publishing Limited Reg. No. 5293401

A CIP catalogue record for this book is available from the British Library

ISBN 978 1 78463 199 4 (Paperback edition)

Typeset in Sabon by Salt Publishing

Printed and bound in Great Britain by Clays Ltd, Elcograf S.p.A

In memory of my dad, Viv and Marie.

This collection is for Charlie and Chloe.

Contents

THE SOMNAMBULIST COOKBOOK

Branch Line

There are no men before me.
     I am it.

My grandfather used to tell the tale
of 'The Monkey's Paw'
and drop me between his knees
then he vanished
leaving only a chair.

My other grandfather I never knew
he walked out in the 1930s
leaving a gap in the language of our family.

Now my father has gone
I'm the last line of defence.

A cage has been lifted
and though I can go anywhere I want
I'm trembling, rooted to the spot.

Here comes my son to bury me.

Those Dark Aunts

What happened to all those dark aunts
who leered above me in the pram
smelling of gin, bridge and perm lotion,
whose budgies squawked through afternoons
at oil paintings of doe-eyed children?

Those aunts who slowly vanished
to reappear as background characters
in novels by Graham Greene,
or worse, Patrick Hamilton; backs turned
in red anoraks to the English Channel

or spotted crossing motorway bridges
that know no slip road access,
a cottage hospital for retired nurses,
with location maps printed
to the underside of paving slabs.

It seems to bring to mind railway station lockers
under dim light bulbs,
away from summer drizzle;
paperback lives folded into suitcases,
out-of-print murder mysteries, never to be solved.

Vanishing Act

Who hasn't thought of leaving it all?
Silently climbing out of bed,
slipping on clothes and shoes
before driving the car to some secluded spot
to make it look like suicide.
Saving money on the side so the bank account
looks untouched. Perhaps to start
a new life in Hampshire or some other place
where no one watches the news,
some English county small town
barely touched by culture
where you can run a shop online
and take walks late in the evening.

But something holds you back,
maybe a child's shoe in the hall
or crayon sketch on the refrigerator,
the thought of your parents ageing
unable to comprehend how you up
and vanished, left not a note or even a sign
of being unhappy. How out of character
all this sorry business seems. But that's the point –
to be someone else, to take a name
and lie in some strange bed and watch
the light gather the morning together
slowly forgetting what made you, you;
redacting the love from your memories.

The Somnambulist Cookbook

When I started sleepwalking
my doctor told me to keep
a diary a log or cookbook
of sleep excursions

~

The Somnambulist Cookbook
offers no recipes he said
just guided tours
through thunderstorms
and imaginary shopping malls
sound-tracked by distant rain
and broken-down escalators

~

There is no one is these places I said
just fleeting movements of light
as if jellyfish were swarming
slightly out of sight

or that there was a surface
edges at the edges
a field of backlit mirrors
in a field of buzzing pylons

~

Much like a stethoscope
he said

      Much like a poem
      I said

≈

Boom-bm goes the iamb of my heart
wiggle your toes offbeat the doctor says

my feet are beastly boys
wanting to run run run

≈

The doctor removes the stethoscope
there is good news he says and there is bad

Do you operate heavy machinery? he asks
I suggest he takes my BMI

≈

When I walk at night I sometimes go
from room to room like a shadow
good says the doctor
we are making progress

≈

In a previous life I was a wall in Spain
they lined men up against me
and shot them one by one

The doctor stands in the corner gently
tapping his head against
the wall

≈

The best way to make dream cake
is to avoid stress by getting ingredients
months in advance

Let them settle into you as if you were a sofa
and they were a fat man

≈

In the land of the blind
the one-eyed man is king

In the land of the somnambulist
we have emperors

≈

I am a city in which dreams walk
they pass each other like clichés
without saying hello

Sometimes they ascend in beautiful glass elevators
to observe the panoply of me
other times they sleep in a skip
and piss themselves

~

The Somnambulist Cookbook
cannot be borrowed from the library
it cannot be bought
it is not available in e-book format
you can only lend it to yourself

Oops! Something went wrong
we cannot find the book you are looking for

~

The practice of everyday life asks of us:
What are our lines of desire?

Will you keep to the paths that civic society
gifted us or pop across the grass?

Ah!
To solve that question
brings the doctor in his long coat
running over car parks
(He remembers when this was all fields)

~

Doctor

my Uncle Dennis was a geography teacher one
summer night he took the boys out beneath
the pylons with strip bulbs that lit up from the
radiation

Doctor, why do they flicker when I walk beneath
them?

~

Never wake a sleepwalker
for it is rude to wake the undead

I ain't no Lady Macbeth
come to admit no murder

not yet

~

The Somnambulist Cookbook
can be passed down the family line

but keep it quiet, let it hum in the drawer
like a bumblebee in a jam jar
let it be tinnitus when you sleep

≈

When you sleep you swallow spiders
when you sleepwalk you swallow
blueprints of unbuilt rooms

Right now I am in the room
that last night was a casino

I was dragged from the tables
kicking and screaming

≈

The doctor likes a smoke
his trails spook the air
and lead me like a mutant rat
through my own labyrinth

I drag my bloodied club through the sand
he is trying to fly

≈

The doctor is away for the holiday season
I send him postcards from the night

I notice them on his return
there are shards of them
in the fire grate

His daughter has laryngitis
so too my postcards, I say

~

The doctor has given me medication
I walk through amber in my days
and tread water in my sleep

How do you feel? asks the doctor
to someone at the edge
of my vision

Oh pretty good
I hear him say

~

This is my double:
he has a firm handshake
and a way with the ladies
tells a good anecdote at dinner

He has centred himself in my bed
pushes my daughter on the swing
feels embarrassed that we wear the same clothes

≈

Now I only call at night

My double has changed the locks
altered the height of my bike saddle
stopped the automatic dial-up
to the pizza parlour

I knock on the mirror glass
he throws water over the surface

I melt away into the corners
he mops furiously

≈

I knock on the doctor's door
he opens it and looks about
before closing it again

[11]

I sit amongst *Country Life*
and *National Geographic*
sniffing his cigarette
stumping in the ashtray

My double enters and goes right in

~

The somnambulist is an orbital motorway
he must shed selves at interchanges
lose complexity in spaghetti junctions
sometimes go at 55 mph

He must be wary of hitch-hikers
and avoid undercooked eggs
in roadside cafés

He must remember that on the continent
they sleep on the right

~

There is speck on the horizon that alters census
figures and there is many a dog howling in the
well as there are balloons stuck in trees which
is to say that there is not that many but enough
to increase the misery quotient of the world to
the nth degree which is in essence why I think I

am cured which is to say it is time for both us
to climb out of the well and float over the trees
until we are specks on the horizon and numbers
in the Office of National Statistics no longer
howling but chasing our tails round and round in
unmedicated joy

The doctor waves his hand
This could be goodbye he says

~

Someone said they saw me walking
across the bypass bridge a few nights back
but they were mistaken

I thought I saw myself down at the railway sidings
as I came in on the late night train
but it was just my reflection

I found myself in the conservatory one night
I was tiny so I stood on myself to get over the wall

~

I have got over myself as if I were a wall
and now I am in the garden sipping gin
and lemonade in the swing chair
above the freshly laid crazy paving

where I buried
The Somnambulist Cookbook

~

The doctor is an untidy man, says his cleaner.
The doctor is a man with poor dental hygiene,
says his toothbrush. The doctor is a man of few
words, say his letters. The doctor is a man who
knows his eggs, say his chickens. The doctor is a
marvellous man, says his bow-tie to the mirror.
The doctor is man of important stature, says his
Mercedes. The doctor is a man with sharp ears,
says his stethoscope. The doctor is a man who
is late to bed early to rise, say his cotton rich
pillows. The doctor is a man of many talents,
says his squash club membership card. The
doctor is an impatient man, say his patients. The
doctor is a tired man, say his eyes

Zzz, says the doctor. Melt, say the ice cubes in
his Johnnie Walker.

A Guide to Being Dead in an English Hotel

1) **Dealing with things**
There is something you have lost. Names evade
you, the ability to understand touch, the French
word for apple. The leaves of a birch distort the
light, they shadow like a school of minnows,
current the room, disturb the still from your
thoughts.

2) **Understanding the strange**
The strangeness of the English hotelier with his
collection of model trains and overweight cats
has made you forget exactly why you are here,
and which you, you are today.

Just accept you are an empty envelope that can be
used again and again.

3) **Not Worrying**
Scribbled notes in the bumper jotter margins
offer clues, but what use are clues if no one apart
from the living are interested in solutions?

You've lost something; that is all – so why
worry?

4) Accepting it

There are a couple arguing in the depths of the hotel; bass notes rise up the legs of the bed. The toothbrush vibrates with words as if called to action.

These things no longer need concern you. It's just noise made by those that are. You are not.

5) Seeking closure

Spatial practice has reduced the size of the room by centimetres. No doubt it used to be bigger, of that you are sure, when you laid here before in love, when you could feel the space around you as a lung and you were a pair of Christmas trees embedded in its bronchi.

Stop holding your breath. That air is no longer yours to breathe.

6) Moving on

Outside, flows of civic society rush past the window and you realise you are losing the city person by person. It is colder in the room. Soon you will rise to embrace your departure.

Everyone Loves a Mystery

Let's run away and hide in the edgelands,
communicate our existence by flashing broken
wing mirrors, use wings of dead bird to point the
way to hastily assembled encampments. We'll
forage off wild mushrooms, hunt mammals
amongst smashed screens and fly-tipped rubble.
The storms in summer time will be dramatic,
the white glow of road-stained ragwort, spear
thistle and dock, washing off with heavy drops.
We'll shelter in forgotten caravans, oddly happy
beneath spaghetti junctions.

Our families will go from door to door,
appear on the six o'clock news and in tears,
implore us to come home, or for some unknown
to let us go. But in time they'll repair: their
neighbours will look them in the eye in the
supermarket aisle, ask how an uncle is, how they
rid the clematis of greenfly. No longer will they
jump when the phone rings, or think about all
the dog walkers out there who might discover us
crudely left beside a quarry under tarpaulin.

There will be sightings of course. Leaking
colours of our last movements on shop cameras,
significant developments linked to lay-bys, one of
us spotted in Clacton-on-Sea, an orange Cortina
sighted in the vicinity. Then the lost-and-should-
know-betters: an irruption of waxwings will be
taken as a sign, papers will talk to a lady with a

vision of us connected to a railway line, flecks of spray paint, cold case connections, spotted with our heads turned in hallway mirrors.

Eventually our faces will fade on telegraph poles, we'll be reduced to ribbon on notice boards, our names faint echoes in village halls, while the flow of traffic around us never dims. No doubt I'll be the first to go – emphysema linked to clogged exhausts. Then lay me low in the lea, lay me down beside winding streams, among bleeding oil-drums and bewildered cattle. Pile up the asphalt pebbles my love. Take us home, you'll hymn with the motorway, take us home.

Pacific Rim

Natalie says, her uncle's dead
In Sydney, and her mother's driven
South all night to be beside
The bed where his body now resides

In time the family will decide
On where his things will end up
Church bazaars and backyards
To be rummaged through by wrinkled hands

Fountain pens, precious gems
The ashtray on the mantelpiece
His fridge still stacked with beers
Lettuce leaves browning at the edge

Long before he died, he once described
The coming taste of death, he said it:
Tastes of ink and copper zinc
And a little bit like Diet Coke

If there's a sound that'll bring me to my knees
It's the birdsong from some distant tree
If the world's a girl, then she is waving
So forlornly from the shore

And if there's one thing I've never seen
It is waves breaking the Pacific Rim
Oh well he said, it seems I'll have to die
Beneath stars over my own backyard

I Slept & Woke to Find Someone Beside Me

It was an old colleague who had escaped the morgue
she was confused and thought I was her husband
and now she wanted me to lie down beside her on the bed.
Her blouse, patterned with meadow flowers
glowed with sunlight flitting through her empty ribcage.
She caught me staring. *Look*, she said,
we're on holiday, don't ruin things,
let's make the best of it.

I held her, what else could I do
as I examined her hair and wondered if it still grew?
As we listened to the wind whistle through her torso
she turned to her side, placed my hand
upon her hollow breast and said
My love, my love, can you hear the sea?

You Took My Ear & Ruined it

after promising me the earth in the empty pool
behind your house. It won't hurt you said
it will look pretty with silver rings and such
and is much easier to pierce once detached.
So I let you and now wonder why,
clasping my hand to the hole in my head.

I am dizzy I think, can hardly hear.
I knock at your door, tape in hand,
ask for it back, explain how it stings
from the wind, how conversations
sound like drownings, that wild animals
come close to the house at night.

What is this? Are my eyes open and seeing? You point
to the garden. Your dog lies amongst half chewed ears.

I Drove Through the Soft Estate

where we simulated drowning in your parent's garage
and for a moment you said you had died.
We asked you to recount and you said the dead
gather at bus stops to eat chips.

You were killed overtaking a coach
in your Vauxhall Corsa. Your parents took home
your rap tapes in a Sainsbury's carrier bag
and hang the Magic Tree every birthday.

At a sixth-form memorial, they played the tapes
and there was an over-dub of a radio show
you had made in your bedroom. Someone bandied 'miracle';
but I couldn't help but think you'd be furious.

At the same function, Sarah Miles
read a poem. It was very different to this.

Come In, Come In

The copper beech is purple wet
        Where were you when your parents met?
   Out the back, putting out a fire?
Down in the willow garden, plucking out a feather?
    No, no, no little girl
       This is the dead time of your life
       Look how the water runs
       How the kitchen clock is stuck
          Someone paused by the back door
And is forever gone
         Churchill on the mantelpiece
      Smashed to smithereens
This is the dead of your life
      Where words died and awoke
      The jam doughnut stuffed in the pocket
        Covered now with ants
A petticoat left in a forest, dangling on a branch
   Musty faced father with cunt on his lips
      Stares at the copper beech
        Reaching out for him
        A peel of bells, a campanile treat
     Says, *come in my child, come in, come in*
       You pause by the doorway
        Ready to enter
To leave placenta rotting on an English lawn
     Mothers call their children home
           The swallows dive for flies

The Mist they Make

I'd like to talk about the rain as if it were a person.
It might be called Elsa or Ryan and live in the Midlands
and have multicoloured fly-strip on the back door
to keep out the green-bottles and the blue in June
July and August. Elsa would sit on cool afternoons
and long for thunder. Ryan would watch the static
of TV channels he doesn't have, and listen to the voices
of the dead speak about how they miss the feel of him
or how satisfying a cigarette is after precipitation;
how they miss the smell of Elsa upon warm pavements
which always makes her feel something even though all lovers
have told her that. It's the mist they make, Ryan and Elsa,
that people forget, when they blot out the rest of the world
and all you can see is them, smudged and sleepy eyed;
their hands moving across your paused moment.

How to Take a Late Train Home

find a compartment
of like-minded travellers
so you know you are safe

if you are a reader
herd with other books

if you prefer earphone bleed
find a blood bank

～

gather yourself together
before your sleep is tethered

draw your bag against your chest
zip the pocket where your wallet rests

you never know, you never know, you never know
whisper the sleepers below

～

the physicality of your sleeping body
will find the rhythm of the journey:

you are flung through time
a defenestrated
cuckoo clock and just as dead

therefore if your head lolls
ensure it falls on sympathetic
shoulders

≈

when you dream on the train
try not to dream of being on a train

instead master the art
of seeing beautiful naked people
who sing softly to you

≈

there are sometimes streaks of light
embers on an aerodrome
lonely farmsteads and motorway
lights fighting the inevitable

that which is inevitable is no business
of yours this late at night

≈

tickets please, tickets please

sorry sir; this ticket is for another day

only kidding! I told you not to dream
of being on a train

                    ~

every memory of a train is of the interior
the buttoned cloth and tea trolley rattle
headless father's leaning out of windows
priests rattling their rosaries

well, that's your memory

looky here
who is this headless man come to join us?

                    ~

murmurs on the inter-city
murmurs on the branch line
murmurs in this little ditty
some delays upon the line

more time to dream more time to sleep
among the postcodes you can't keep

                    ~

when we get to terminal town
before we alight from the carriage
(but stand much too early)
avoid eye contact with others

let this company be an accident
a shared moment of the unspoken

don't look back at the discarded news
the crisp packets and drained beer
they are just the archaeological remnants
of the 22:30 out of Liverpool Street

~

the man at the ticket gate is your favourite char-
acter / he is one gene off handsome and looks like
a roadie for Gallon Drunk / he sometimes comes
to your dreams with his hair slicked back / his
sparse moustache clinging like seaweed to the
rock pools of his face / he tells of a place beyond
the terminal where the trains keep running / an
elaborate network of tunnels under the city that
connect the old lime pits / here there is a secret
society that will one day throw off the fettered
manacles of neo-liberalism and introduce the
utopia of Thomas More / It will be a macro-
economic miracle of endogenous growth marvels
/ the swallows will sing on the wind and the rivers
will flow to the seas with renewed vigour

You are working too much. Your brain is flat-lining. It's dying man, dying!

≈

I survived the late train home you say
        to the metered taxi driver
praying for red lights.

≈

and you get home and you say *ah I am home! It's good to be home*, you will kiss your sleeping child on the head before heading to bed to the warmth of your wife but the warmth is not there tonight and someone has left a dead wolf in the bed of your lovely daughter and when you get home you will say, *ah I am home. Home is good, home is my altar so let me fall to my knees* and you will kiss your dead child on the head before heading to bed to the warmth of the wolf who ate your wife and wears her

≈

when I get home?

oh look, you've just woken up
still on the train.

Mr Litnanski

What are you but remnants from around the house?
Unidentified objects that once belonged to something
else. I hear the over-winding of the musical boxes
in your wheeze, it's not Swan Lake and it's not Erik
Satie. It's the off tune wind through a bullet hole.
What will they do with all your stuff but skip the lot.
The horse brasses, donkey ring holders, the hidden
page three's grinning with yellowed tits from behind
your TV, the curtains that honk of pipe tobacco
and Saturday night sweet and sour. Your history is
one of plastics, badly positioned patio stones, hours
spent on the ring road in traffic jams with a car radio
you never could fix. But you had your days, selling
tickets up the picture palace, the girls wet with rain,
smudged eyes all heading into the dark to watch some
film about life elsewhere. Holidays down in Brighton,
lying about business plans to avoid sitting on your
own in the breakfast room while loud mouthed
Northern families laid waste to the breakfasts. The
union days and the social club, where a fight could
break out and you'd wade in, nothing like a crack
to the jaw, someone's tooth in your beer; what were
those years but railway lines all leading in the same
direction across the junction of your pigeon chest?
Little trains in the park. You wished you had a son
so you could ride it. You made model planes to give
to your mates to put on top of the washing line poles.
You would often lay in bed on windy summer nights,
listening to the tiny propeller going round, wishing
for all the world it might lift your heart.

Nostalgia

In the end of my head is a place I want to forget,
the place where I misremember whole summers,
where pylons are beautiful as we wade
through cornfields up to our waists,
backlit by a coming storm, as it's always hot here,
where, in the radio crackles, a tired voice sings
about wild swimming, and I daydream of coach trips
through the Pyrenees; here in this oubliette of memory
I am happy, I have a full head of hair
and girls come with smiles on their lips
to tenderly hover their hands centimetres
from the skin of my back, they are always laughing
and wear dresses with meadow flowers;
look, there's Georgina before she rolled her car,
stroking the saddle of my bicycle, Penny is smoking
a cigarette, worldly Penny, tap-tapping her ash
into the tributary of the Darent, as Gen leads a pony
to the water's edge, but stays on the far side,
raises one arm; I wave back, thumbs poke
through the cuffs of my jumper, minnows stalk the shallows,
everyone is on holiday, the house always empty,
ghosts collect in my breathing, flowers grow dirty
along the edges of the roads. Fuck you nostalgia, Fuck you.

Notes Towards Being an Adult

A

Sometime last week I suddenly realised I had been alive
for a long time. Before it was simple. I was a kid, then I was not.
Now I am something else. I want to tell you about light,
but there is so much spent light that I don't know where to begin.
A caravan sales yard. The Hole of Horcum. Michelle Merritt's red hair
and blue nurse's uniform, her tiny watch so erotic.
All were in the light at different times. All are dead moments.
I try to order the different people I have been, friends I have had
and lost to other cities, or just lost, their letters
to me about life in Shanghai, Saint-Étienne, or even Hatfield
badly filed in a plastic box in the garage.

B

I am now in the time of my life I used to try to imagine when I was seven
or eight. How will I look? I thought. Sometimes I'd catch a reflection
in the dirty train window that would prematurely age me, and I'd see
a sweaty man with stuck down hair and fear. I have lost the sequence of
    things,
now memories amalgamate into a mush of moments that I am not sure
I lived any of it. That watch was so erotic. Graduation was weaker
than enrolment. Some girlfriends still give me a little kick to the heart,
but not the ones I'd expected. Sometimes a nameless face will come out
of the dark on the back of a pony and say: '*Come on Steve, let's go
to the drive-through, let's laugh in the gap between the pictures of
    the food
and the reality, before we realise there is no such thing as irony.*'

C

Vladmir Putin will not read this, even so, there are people
that I do not wish to offend for the sake of self-preservation
as I enjoy Coca-Cola in Barcelona without the risk of polonium
(and even linking the two things might be risqué in the 21C.)
As I also enjoy my liberty to walk down a Parisian high street
with my head still in conversation with my torso. It's this sense
of preservation which has helped me avoid situations some gain thrills
from, even if I have risked suffocation between the legs of others
or simply ridden my bicycle into a post avoiding a pedestrian.
I guess it's a life half lived if you wish to be unkind. Go ahead
I have no fear of offending you. You are radiant tonight. Lovely.

D

My father can name all the fields and woods of the village
he has lived in since birth; which was April 1934. He knows
houses by the names of the dead, who were farm workers
or print workers down at the old mill. But now come new comers:
Londoners, looking for the rural idylls, sound-tracked by the M25.
They call the recreation ground the park; the meadows are now
the tow-path. *It's OK* I say to my incredible shrinking father
amongst the disappearing lives that leave the indelible marks
of change on his face; *they used to be something else before you came
    here*
and they will be something else again. No! says my mother
from behind her roast beef, *I will fight them every step of the way!*

E

rguments are pointless unless used as an excuse for 'hot sex',
hich citizens of the world have very different notions of.
once said she loved a good argument and I knew then
   would never work, even though she didn't fancy me anyway.
's not the confrontation that jars but the waste of words that pile up
 the corners of the room, letters left as dead flowers in vases no one
      wanted.
oo ashamed to sweep them up, they fester and rot until someone
athers them up and puts them back under the tongue. I tried an argument
nce, it was about money and I lost. There are many can of worms
      unopened.
store them in the cupboard, listen to them writhe as I fall asleep.
omeone is keeping note for what can only be described as a rainy day.

F

here are many erotic things in this world if you look hard enough;
leeves half rolled was one I was told that could excite a girl from Telford,
ttle flashes of longing is what it's all about. A mole or the way you sneeze
ould offer the way to coupling of some sort. Coupling is still a mystery
      for adults
e seem to all have different ideas on who or what is superfluous to our
      needs
r if sugar or television is bad for us. I sometimes like to be alone in the
      cinema
nd forget that I am a coupler, and I could be sixteen or seventy
   really doesn't matter, as in the auditorium dark I can cease to exist

for a brief time, and feel what it is like to not be needed, to be with other
    ghosts
in a little boat of a Monday afternoon. Just a bit out of time, that's all I
    need
to return happy to the shore of some pretty feet, just poking out of the
    duvet.

G

Everything comes back to G. It's a good note to end on.
I sometimes hit a minor key and lose my way in the pattern.
L on the phone; L on her favourite beach. What silly things
to do in time, when there seems so much of it. The sea was lovely
in a snowy way. The pines were cold pylons humming in the mist.
She kept crying. What can you do? You can't comfort someone
who hates you in that moment. What are these moments but excursions
into difficulty with an idiot at the wheel? I can't find my way out,
of these relived moments, but instead I carry them like a man
heading out of town, coat pockets weighted down by heavy stones.

Anglia Square

Of your fearful symmetry I was afraid. I was young then, and could only relate you to houses covered in Christmas lights, a dog dragging its backside across a carpet, a man hiding in the leylandii. Now, you are much more the slant of light in a shady room, the wind-farm out to sea, the echo on a school field. Oh you wounded beast! You council designated demolition job! There are fragments of love messages caught in your barbwire. I will read some to you: *'Potatoes 2, XXL'*, *'Quavers for the baby'*, *'. . . the thing I can't remember'*. Or how about this: *'I hear the Police dogs howling in the spiral stairs.'* Further out, signs of *diss-respekt* plastered on the walls, **ATL CREW, IN YER MANNER.** Far cry from the planners who dreamed of you as a town within a city; a concrete and glass perplex, with Hollywood cinema, the cardboard Wookie and droids, guardians of a future discarded like a fag packet. In your centre a little train follows a circular track, a man with a placard stands and speaks in your voice to the pigeons, *'entropy, entropy, they've all got it in for me'*. The car tyres scream in your upper reaches; dirty puddles reflect the endless, ambivalent blue, I stand and stroke you like a stranded whale on a wintered beach. I whisper in your ear like a child: *'Sleep now mister whale, sleep now and dream no more.'*

Wasted Afternoons

The remains of your twenties are spent in waste
/ hangovers with their various chocolate bars /
cigarettes stubbed on last night's take away /
ash and kebab / the cocktail of the single man
who spends his day off on a Wednesday in some
provincial town which only makes the news every
few years / you have a pizza in the fridge about
to go off / it's been there since last Tuesday / you
only bought it as the girl at the till once told you
she liked your T-shirt, but she wasn't there and
you're getting around to thinking about the oven
/ the TV is on and the stylus clicks in the run out
groove but today is different / the days of waste
are coming to an end / half-hearted half-naked
you flick through a music magazine / a univer-
sity peer stares back at you from her rock outfit
fêted by critics everywhere / for 23.4 minutes you
really stare at a single cypress poking over the
house opposite

      it never seems to move

  ants scurry along the sill
       a telephone rings next door

Someone opens the serving hatch in your head
hands a bunch of lilies / screams into your face

The Mouth Ulcer

You slip with the toothbrush, ramming it into the gum. A day or so later, it is an enormous mouth ulcer. Most foods are agony. You think about the mouth ulcer most of the day. It is hard to kiss your baby daughter, and even harder your wife. She will later go through your texts, suspicious that you didn't want to kiss for longer. You did try to explain about the mouth ulcer at least three times, but it never registered. At night, disturbed by the soreness, you wake up intermittently. The sky is edging itself through the bottom of the curtains in a blue hue that you recognise to be 4 a.m. There are boxes in your hypnopompic state, which have a certain way of being carried. You fail every-time and wake up with each of these failures. There were moments where you forgot about the pain. There was a man at the bus stop, you remember him as he was wearing shorts and a radio which was clamped to his left ear. He had breasts that hung down with lines of long hair, only two or three maybe, and his belly was bright pink from sunburn. He didn't notice you pass, he was talking about tables to the radio which was playing so loudly it was distorting. The music was woozy, like something heard through the floor of a ferry in 1929. A little later, you see him again on the bus as it passes. It seemed to slow down so you could catch sight of him. He stared out the window as if it were one way glass. *He has a rich history of ulcers,* you say, *and keeps a record on the back of dropped railway tickets*. The ulcer now has a ridge, like a membrane, the lip is curling away from itself. You try steamed courgette, dappled cheese, unsalted aubergine, but it's still so painful. To make matters worse, someone has replaced your peppermint tea with Yorkshire tea, and the black soup is foul, lacking in the anaesthetic that you crave. This time next week it will be cleared up, forgotten about. But you'll run your tongue over the lumpen skin and feel something a bit like loss.

Spoiler

I fell asleep with the TV on
and caught the end of John Carpenter's
The Thing featuring The Original Shatner
cast of *Star Trek* who were under attack
from a tentacled blob,
whose mouth resembled the shape
of a train tunnel, into which Shatner
threw a fire extinguisher, so the blob
exploded covering them in jelly
and they ran to their space ship
before the complex fell apart
and they had special suits for the G-Force
created by the spinning ring
that was actually their craft
and as the ring started to spin
Shatner noticed that a small boy
hadn't fastened his suit,
and was hanging dangerously
towards certain death,
so Shatner unstrapped and leapt,
grabbing the boy, and with perfect
judgement landed back on his suit,
into which he placed the little lad
which of course meant that Shatner
now faced certain death, but heroes
when they die just close their eyes,
but as he did so, you noticed
he was changing into a blob,
and, what a twist, he was going to infect
all the people of planet earth, as a blob

could probably handle 12G's easily,
and then the film finished and I know
it had ended, as when I woke again
it was late night snooker,
the one played by dogs.

Today I enter my thoughts
on *rottentomatoes.com*
'I can't wait to see *The Thing* again
it's not as scary as I thought
and it's good to see the old gang
back together, one last time.'

Ha Ha Ha

I awake from a dream laughing, to find you laughing too. What's funny I said. Not much you said still fast asleep. We are keeping our jokes from each other, I think. The pigeons have yet to come and it is still night and I have a belly full of wind. Into the dark of the flat I go. The trees outside are still, the canary in his cage is still. The little bird is a like a puppet waiting to be animated. The leaves are like the set waiting to shake or be backlit. This is all pretence I think. I go back to bed. The thing in my dream that made me laugh was about petunia oil I say. There was this man all masculine, but he slapped himself with petunia and it smelt like rotting moss on a fire. In the dark I wonder what made you laugh. If you ask a sleeper a question sometimes they answer you, I think. I ask you and you answer: I asked your Mother what she misses about her children and she answered their handwriting . . . I don't know why I found it funny, maybe it was the look upon your face? Ha Ha Ha I think, Ha Ha Ha.

Carole

It's 1994, I've just turned 17. Nothing to do
during the school holidays when I'm not at
Sainsbury's pushing trolleys around to 'Modern
Life is Rubbish' in my head, but to hang out in
the fields near the cottage hospital above the
A21. Paul warns of ravers who might appear at
any time and have no sympathy for our fashion
sense. My hair is long, shoulder length and curly
blonde. I'm interested in a girl named Carole who
looks a bit like Mark Keds, the lead singer of the
Senseless Things, who is androgynous, so it's ok.
We hang out and smoke Royals as there's 24 in
a packet. I think Carole smokes too, but not as
much. Sometimes she foregoes which makes her
more mysterious. She has a boyfriend, Simon
Laszlo. He doesn't like me much, we never meet.
Once, on stage with my band, I performed in
bare-feet and he took one of my Converse and
hid it behind a curtain. I never found it and went
home with one shoe, hopping to the transit van.
Simon is tall and lanky, he too has long hair but
he's under attack from acne. Mine isn't too bad I
reason; most of the time it hides politely behind
the hair. I always like to wear my Screamadelica
T-shirt when I visit Carole, as she's commented
on it. We wear friendship bracelets and watch
the moths under the Victorian street lamp in the
middle of the field. I try to write poems about
moths and lamp posts, as it produces a longing I
can't put my finger on, but ultimately the poems

always lead back to Carole. In the end, I take it too quickly in a tent near Plaxtol. I never really see Carole again, only at the edge of the local indie scene, though I always see her, in the morning mist on the farm where we camp, looking lost amongst my friends, looking at me as if I were a stranger, her deciding to walk back the eight miles to Tonbridge with Paul as chaperone. I'm sorry Carole, I try to say, too ashamed in my Screamadelica T-shirt and goose bumped skin.

Peepo!

Sometimes, when you look at me closely
or an object for the first time
I see someone I last saw twenty years ago.
See them line up, the old devils
to briefly light upon your face
you unaware as your father scrutinises
a smile, a simple gesture
or something you do with the hands.

Perhaps it's a game of roulette,
the ball will drop as the wind will change
and leave you stuck with a particular face
staring back like they've just stepped out
of some time machine. The stairs my little love
are getting steeper. Hold on tightly. Help me.

I Have to Say this Before We Go Any Further

There are things I have to shape in the ice
in the back of beyond, in the touching of our arms
against the way we look into each other's eyes.
I have to remember that it is you
not my idea of you, not my desire of you
but you, you with the big eyes of blue
the eggshell blue of delicate spinning saucers
(here I go again, hopeless and poetic).

I have to say no, I am meant to say no
but the tired bee I rescued on the petrol forecourt
is looking up at me and saying *come on son*
come on boy, she wants you and you need to tell her
and I'm saying what the fuck do you know?
You're just a bee.

Hand Writing

Just some scrap paper, nothing important or too clever:
a shopping list, a note to my mother, just something
in scrawl, the letters nervously making their way
across the skin of paper with gaps like lost milk teeth
where anything could get through and vanish forever;
the intricate patterns of campanology; a song you would sing;
the class number of vintage tractors; even now I want to sway
with cardiographic consonants, vowels with a clumsy tenderness
    beneath.

Instead it is the odd slant of 'Rew' in a birthday card
which floors me with its sudden attack. It once held
£20 which was more precious then, and if I am honest
I may have even paid scant attention to the rest.
Now it's your handwriting, the letter's elaborate charms
which carries your voice back to me; a lamb in a child's arms.

Closing Time

'The British Pub Association says up to 29 pubs close every week in the UK.' BBC News

I

Ring the bell in The Shortbread St
Ring the bell in The Bubble and Squeak
Ring the bell in The Crown & Thistle
Ring the bell in The Pig & Whistle
Ring the bell in The Kitten in the Weir
Ring the bell in The Gay Grenadier
Ring the bell in The Burnt Down Mill
Ring the bell in The Bunkers Hill
Ring the bell in The Bird Bath Inn
Ring the bell in The Rubber Ring
Ring the bell in The Bow-Wow-Wow
Ring the bell in The Calfless Cow
Ring the bell in The Cambridge Boffin
Ring the bell in The Wooden Coffin

Fat man with Cornish pasty, bottom lip quivers with dribble, *it's here*, he says, pushing the side plate with wheat and flying birds over the sticky varnish, *it's fresh* he says, straight from the microwave, here it is, this half-moon of pastry and unidentified animal parts in the worst pub in the village where you can pour yourself a cheeky half when the landlord is up the other end puffing on his JPS, here it is sans salad, with ketchup solidifying while you wait and Dire Straits queue behind Blue Oyster Cult who gave way to Dexys and no one chalks their name above the pool table and your stomach turns from the bad beer and you say *I wouldn't change it for the world as pubs are the life of the village.* Cars sometimes slow to see if there are lunches. Landlord stares at them as they pass, calls them names under his breath. The village is haunted by empty saloon bars and this pasty, cooling in the English air, sinking back into itself.

Welney

Suddenly East Anglia is green again. The silver green of barley fields, the tufty green of meadows broken by the yellow remains of last year's rushes, the square woods of field boundaries, the new leaves lighter green, the crude plastic blue of a distant Portaloo for field workers, a celestial apartment, a Fenland Tardis.

A year shuffling back and forth between cities on a near empty train, through small towns starting to wake up, isolated fen houses like embargoed ships tethered to the landscape, and everyday there is something new, and the country like the city is always changing, nothing is ever finished, things seemingly disappear.

So it goes, moment to moment, seemingly random. What do you do with the space they leave, the gap where a building once stood, the place where there used to be a huge apple tree? Light fills it, the moment is new, yet loss interferes with each moment; gives it a shape like one of those magic eye pictures of dolphins appearing from garish fractals.

You stare too long and you see more than you want to. So you have to shake it off, a dog shaking the scent of a stranger's hand. There are things to be done, emails to answer, tickets to show, books to be read, essays to mark. The landscape is just green, it is morning, space is simply filled with light.

Come On You Thing of Worry & Fuck With Me

Oh you thing of sleeplessness, you fucker of the mind
you are people without pushchairs taking the elevator
and I want to take your formless face and smash it
into my knee, into me, to be part of me, like a wart of love
that I can scare children with, my witch's nipple
of soured milk, dates missed, replies expected
warnings to the curious

       You fucking nasty raiser of the heartbeat
dryer of throats and tightner of sphincters,
you brown envelopes through the letter box
wearing private and confidential like a monster
wearing the heads of men around its neck
and beating your chest for the meal to come
you stalker of the margins, you speeding executive
I want to drown you in your own sea
step on your head to get on the boat and wave at you
as you flounder in the water

                       but see you come
see you come quickly through the shitty detritus
of my life to climb back into the boat
and throttle me with the cords of deadlines
throttle me if you dare because I'm ready for you
even though you wear my face and hold my mistakes;
a flashlight coming closer from the depths of rest

Acknowledgements

Poems in this collection have previously been published in or association with, *Butcher's Dog, Ink, Sweat and Tears, Under the Radar* and The York Mix Poetry Competition.

Thanks to:

George Szirtes, Laura van Ree; The Butchery Poetry Group Past and Present: Tiffany Atkinson, Martin Figura, Jo Guthrie, Chris Hamilton-Emery, Nathan Hamilton, Andrea Holland, Matthew Howard, Helen Ivory, Esther Morgan, Jon Morley and Tom Warner; Meirion Jordan and all at Gatehouse / Lighthouse; Tom Corbett; the Dark Aunts: Michaela Nettell, Abi Dagleish, Kel Robb and Lorna Shipley; Tom Simmons, Phil Archer, and Russell Wickwar; Jon Baker and Sian Croose and all the passengers of the Voice Project. Huge thanks to David Evans.

This book has been typeset by
SALT PUBLISHING LIMITED
using Sabon, a font designed by Jan Tschichold
for the D. Stempel AG, Linotype and Monotype Foundries.
It is manufactured using Holmen Book Cream 70gsm,
a Forest Stewardship Council™ certified paper from the
Hallsta Paper Mill in Sweden. It was printed and bound
by Clays Limited in Bungay, Suffolk, Great Britain.

CROMER
GREAT BRITAIN
MMXIX